Taking A Look Around

Taking A Look Around

Gabriel Anthony Lopez

Blue Ink Media Solutions

Taking A Look Around

Printed in the United States of America
ISBN 978-1-967279-48-7 (hc)
ISBN 978-1-967279-46-3 (sc)
ISBN 978-1-967279-47-0 (e)

06.02.2025

This book is printed on acid-free paper.

Blue Ink Media Solutions
1111B S Governors Ave
STE 7582 Dover,
DE 19904

www.blueinkmediasolutions.com

Table of Contents

Angered January

Cold, wind
In a bind
Need to go home
I have something to grind

My mind isn't at ease
In case you didn't know
I don't say please
Nor do I appease

Snow
It's too low
It drags me down
When it melts, I could drown

Blow sideways today
Maybe on Monday, I'll get back up
But for now, I stay down
I smile only politely to the crown

No More War

No more war
Here we go
With you by the pool
Intervention is needed or not
Calling my name
Tonight is dazzling with you
Socialism is coming
I don't know if we can pull it off
Decadents, we are
Capitalism is no more
What are we to do

No more war
Here we go
With you by the pool
Intervention is needed or not
Calling my name
Tonight is dazzling with you
Dystopia or Utopia, I see in your eyes
Wretchedness is not me
No more sardonic anger
The cynicism I am, maybe
I feel these monsters are in the future
But right now, I am with you

Lauding their names
I feel so cold
You are in my soul
The faster I go, the more I see you
There we go
I win; let's go

Petra

Pink stone
Alone speaking
To the nomads
Through a lighted passage

Dusty ancient murals
Now seen with their laurels again
Befitting of an emperor
One day, I will be

Up the steep hill, I climbed
To see where the genies walk
Compass pointing
I placed it on the rock

Knees locking, I looked around.
Only to find a friend with a smile
Took a picture, then winked at me, the traveler
She was from somewhere beyond in the East

Brazil

The inner sanctum of rain
A car rushed by
A hushed murmur from a passerby
With outstretched arms, a new man was there

He said he was on a mountain
Always there
Dare, I visit
Laid bare, my soul would be
Shame is nothing but tragedy

What would I say?
I do not know
A great city is below
Gathering them all, he is but me

I'm from somewhere, he said
I'll never let this wound be
Tossing and turning, I did one night
Only to find emptiness everywhere

Egg

Nested in a memory
It cracked
A long slumber turned into joy
The boy sang a song of remembrance

A call he had heard like none before
With others, he sought refuge
A sorcerer's touch, he felt
It cast a spell to teach him

Another spell was heard in a song
One of grief and pain
He gathered his thoughts
Another day, he wanted
A sorcerer's power

The hour came
He brought his pen out
In the ink he wrote was his might
With a nod, the sorcerer smiled

Chopsticks

At night, with a group of friends
For the first time
Soju and white rice
Jokes and laughter

Fumbling, bashful
Want to know how
Dokdok, they say
If you can keep them apart

Please come here, we say
For more soju
The clock strikes nine
And we still dine

We are ready for the night.
With soju in hand
It is our first time
In this land

Busan Sand

Cool sand
Looking out over the strait
Waves crashing on the beach
Thinking of home

But this is a new home
A day to remember what once was
A party
More friends

Warmth from the Eastern sun
On my face
Fingering the sand
Letting it fall

It was only the beginning of a journey
Already exhausted
Laid out a towel
For a nap

Perhaps another day
Another hour
For a party
But now I wish to rest

On the beach
With sand all around
I love this new town
And this new sun is smiling down

Hiking or climbing?

Before work
I wanted to let go
Up the local mountain
To a new spot to view my new home

It took some time
I met a friend and had a drink
Soju
It was the best I've had so far

We searched around
And around
Looked down and found another path
Wandering into a temple

Pondering what it all means
Small figurines placed in reverence
On a rock
Incense filled the air

Up and through trees we went
To the side of the mountain
Where we wondered, what reverence meant

To one, it affected them deeply,
to the other only so much
It was a pleasant visit
With more to come
Only a tiny day's hike now, it was

Coyote In the Dust

It ran and sprinted
On the other side
Where the quail were
They could hear it coming

Wings beat; feathers flew.
Dust was between the cactuses
It blossomed up to where the desert flowers were
They shuddered

Chasing continued
With a dry mouth
It clamped its mouth around feathers
Now dust

Up the cactuses, the quail went.
Back down into the mesquite
Careful, coyote
Clever and spirited quail
Are there

Over here said the coyote
Birds of this type flock together
Too much, he said
With a subtle touch of his paw,
One fell when cornered
Mother squawked
Quiet filled the field of cactuses
And mesquite

Beaches & Wine

Sea salt on the tip of my tongue
Rays of sunshine
Splashed with water
Over my Body

Deep blue swirled
Ahead, white foam bounced
On my head
A seashell crushed beneath my feet

The sun fell behind the tree line,
Time to go to a vineyard
Dry wine touched my lips
Aged cellars shown

Green leaves and vines
Stretched for what looked
Like miles
Some of the crops were almost in

Mountains are seen
Wine with the upward hills
Markets and streets
Selling the elixir

Sun-tanned skin
Pungent wine gave
Me, a darker tone
The Earth showed its true self

Sea of Galilee

Bursts of sunshine across
The biblical waters
Of calming the tempest
Calling his disciples

Gentle, waves
Soothe
A hardened, traveled soul
Winds blow to the west

A flock of birds
Fly over
Rain falls
It's cool

Pouring, rain
Unforgiving rain
Forgiveness is here
From the god-man
Who called us all

Pressure
The feeling of someone
Walking on water
Baptism by water has come

From the sea of fright
To the calming of the sea
Who is he?
A savior has come

Monkeys

Far from a howler
They are
With small, spidery
Limbs

On a whim, they jump
From tree to tree
They see each other
And us

Stole a hat
And a banana
Up into the trees one went
To share

Once in a while
A call is heard
A roar of the jungle
Not enough to humble

A green jungle
They reside in
They call it home
Partitioned by man

Scientists and researchers come.
In search of their language and culture
Only shoo away the vultures of industry
Remaining the monkeys of the jungle

Snake Eyes

They cut like ice
When you roll the dice
A piercing, unforgiving look
When you roll with snake eyes

Twisting around and around
Through the dirt, grass, and leaves
Caught in the snake's eyes
It is to roll the dice

Waiting in a den
Through fall and winter
Until one day during spring
Warmth from all around
Kindled the fire in the snake's eyes

Out and about it went
To the stream, fresh with melted snow
A wicked glance of an eagle
Met snake eyes

Their eyes met
Unblinking, the snake looked
It was not time to roll the dice
Only when he drew snake eyes

Swooping down from the trees
The eagle almost
Drew snake eyes
Scuttling under a rock
Curled up for safety
It was not the time to come up with snake eyes

Sepulcher

Holiness is there
Death turned to life
Buried then glorified
Prayer to the unseen God

Light through the dome
To the stone
Angelic hymns heard
All to glorify
Motionless, I stand
Hands clasped in prayer
Cool air from somewhere
The tomb is there to behold

The site where he died
In agony
His mother there
Only to see her son die

In three days
He will rise
In time, the darkness rises
Then, it will be divided
And die

Nothing divided stands
His holy hands cross mine
I am united
This time, not for a time
But for unending days until the next time

Dead Sea

Arid, parched
Walking across the sand
To the calm, cool waters of the Dead
Ancient baths took the mud

I throw it on my body.
Enthralled by the feeling of agelessness
I draw more mud
And everyone comes near

Getting to know the water
I remember the unique property
Splash! I went down into the dark water
Mud everywhere, on my face, in my nose

I sprang up from the bottom.
I float there
Like ice in a cup
Like a bug on the water

Laughter heard
As I lay up towards the sun
Floating there, on my back
Waiting for nothing but transformation

With salt in my hair
I joined the fun of splashing the healing water
I plop down on the sand
And watch the sun cast a shadow across the Dead Sea

Jerusalem

In the Old City
There have been ghosts
The Holy Ghost
And the ghost of Him
Doubting everything, I walked the streets
Much like him, he believed
The walls course around
Some gates are open; some are closed

Solemn and quiet
Awe at the Golden Gate
I enter
In trepidation

Stone, cobbled streets
A vendor here and there
A waft of falafel
It's in the air

Different quarters
Separate the faiths
Of Abraham
Pilgrims everywhere

To one quarter
To the next
To their holy sites
They're directed
For their prayers to ascend to heaven

Sphinx

Silent as a lion
As remarkable as a human
It sits there
With power

The Power of the Saharan Sands
Course through its stone
It might as well be veins and
Fur

Sitting there through day and night
Watching over the ancient city
Tombs of the Pharaohs
Release their whispers to it

Guardians of humanity
The great one has sat there
For thousands of years
Only for sand to cover it

Its better half came
And uncovered it.
Welcoming the sunlight
Once again

Now, it is there for the world to see
For history to speak once again
For sands not to mute the mouth of the Sphinx
The lion's roar was heard once again

Barcelona

Pounding techno music
Reverberates in my body
A drink in hand
A dance away from ecstasy

This is the party tonight.
Half forgotten
I am in Barcelona
Where do I stand tonight?

They also say
You're in Spain
So, you might as well
Party your life away

A couple of hours earlier
I was at a marvelous site
The holy family
Of Salvador

Spires turn upward
To the cloudy skies
Rain slips down the façade
Onto the clean streets of the city

I walked inside and
I was amazed by its size
Its beauty
It appeals to the sacred
And the divine
To have that heard again is a blessing

Island Hopping

In the distance, there is a lot of green
Or sandy, brown
With the aqua water surrounding them
The boat guide eases onto the beach

We are on Koh Lipe
Far from the known traveler's tracts
Beige and white beaches
With waves lapping their shores

A breeze eased the
Feeling of humidity
We take off our clothes
And head to the beach

This is not like Koh Tao
My fellow traveler says
Danger may be nearby
An inlet is there for snorkeling

I put down my beach towel
And put on sunscreen
The warmth of the Andaman Sea's sun
Caressing me

I take notice of where I am
Near the end of Thailand
To maybe a new journey
Through Malaysia

Cambodia

Monumental grey stone temples
Faces
Gnarled jungle trees
Saffron-robed monks and deities

Ancient words speak
While walking amidst the ruins
The largest temple
To see Angkor Wat

Long forgotten by time,
But why
Now, it is only meant for tourists
But is it for the best

Hot, jungle days
Roaming through the temples
We worship
And take heed

We hope for blessings
We make offerings
Only to walk amongst
The silent grey stone

Green jungles enclose
The temples
Nestles and keeps it safe
All the while reclaiming what belongs to it
Maybe one day the offerings will be heard

www.ingramcontent.com/pod-product-compliance
Lightning Source LLC
Chambersburg PA
CBHW011226120626
46545CB00010B/3171